Published by Freiling Publishing, a division of Freiling Agency, LLC.

70 Main Street, Suite 23-MEC
Warrenton, VA 20186

www.FreilingPublishing.com

ISBN 9781950948222

Printed in the United States of America

To Paco, the best cat in the whole wide world. Thank you for letting me carry you like a rag doll and for loving me so much. I know you're playing in Heaven...I bet it's beautiful!

Do you know what

grit

means?

Well, my mom says I have it. Having grit means
you keep working towards a goal even when
it's hard. Someone who has grit is fearless
and unstoppable.

Sometimes people ask my mom and dad why I'm different. They ask why I need extra help doing things.

It takes

grit

for me to do things that are easy for most kids, like running fast or putting on a pair of shoes.

Do you want to know why? I'd like for you to put a pair of shoes on for me so you can see what it's like to be me! Let's pretend they are my shoes. My name is Frankie, and here's my story...

When I was born, I was so tiny; I weighed less than a can of beans! That's because I was born eight weeks early. The doctors made me stay in the hospital for a few weeks, covered in wires in this little glass box.

I was finally able to go home to my own
cozy bed and to meet my cat, Paco. My parents thought that all was great until I was five
months old. My mom noticed I wasn't reaching
for toys with my right hand like other babies
do. So they took me to see a doctor, and then
another and another to find out why.

The doctors all agreed that I had cerebral palsy. Those are two big words to describe a baby who has an injury to their brain.

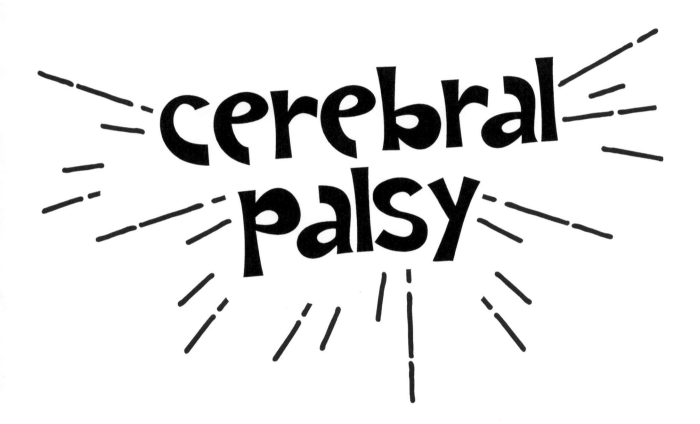

How did I hurt my brain?
Why did this happen to me?

My doctors said I had a
stroke when I was in my
mom's belly. A stroke
happens when blood stops
flowing from our bodies
to our brain. Strokes
usually happen to older
people, but I'm living
proof that babies can
have them too.

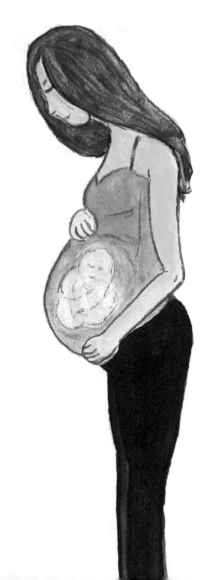

So, after seeing lots of doctors, my parents knew I wasn't going to be like other kids. They were even more determined to give me everything I needed to overcome future challenges. This was when I started going to therapy.

Therapy is a big part of my life, just like gymnastics, ballet, and soccer are for some of my friends. At therapy, I walk on a treadmill, do jump exercises, and lots more.

Sometimes, my brain has a hard time telling my right arm/hand what to do. My therapist puts funny stickers on my right arm and leg that make them tingle. They are connected to a machine that helps my brain spark so that I can move muscles that don't want to move. It's like magic!

Outside of therapy, I still see many doctors today, including a neurologist—that's a big word for a brain doctor. My mom says, "if you bunch all of my doctors together, they are on a team... my team. Team Frankie!"

My team helps me be the strongest and healthiest I can ever be! One of my favorite team members is Dr. Jan.

She's my brain doctor. I love seeing her, and guess what? She has cerebral palsy too. She's very smart, and patients come from all over the world to see her!

Just like most kids, I go to school. When I was three years old, I went to a special preschool. I loved it!

My mom used to call me "the mayor." I didn't know what a mayor was, but after school, I would wave and say hi to every person that passed me, even people in their cars...with their windows rolled up! I guess mayors are super friendly!

As I'm getting older, I don't greet people as often anymore. Sometimes it's hard for me to speak the words I want to say, so I hold them in. I hope my friends know that when they say hi to me, it makes me happy. When I don't say hi back, I'm smiling and waving back at them from my heart.

My favorite subject at school? Music!

Music makes me so happy! I want to be a singer when I grow up. Give me a stage, turn on the tunes, and you can make me do almost anything... fearlessly AND with

grit

I'm usually at the bottom of the stage when I have a performance at school.

That's because my balance isn't that great yet, and everyone wants me to be safe. That's ok though—it gives me more room to DANCE!

Just like my doctor team,
I have another team at
school...I like to call it
a squad. Like a
cheerleading squad!

I have teachers, therapists,
and a special PE coach that
all work together to lift me
up and support me.

I have my friend squad, too. Even though I don't like to ask people for help, I love it when my teachers and friends lend a hand. Remember, not everything is as easy for me, like opening a bag of chips, cutting around fun shapes with scissors, or putting on gloves in the winter.

During the day when I'm in class, a special teacher works side by side with me. This is because I need a little extra help and more time to learn things my friends are learning. On other days a therapist comes into the classroom to get me. Where am I going? Hopefully, not to the principals' office!! I'm either going to see my speech therapist or my physical therapist.

One day after school, my mom asked me, "Why do you stand in one spot during recess?" My teacher must have told her, or maybe my mom was spying on me! It feels like I'm standing there for one minute, not the entire recess. I guess I get stuck in time, watching my friends play during recess doing things I can't do, like the monkey bars. In my heart, I feel joy because I imagine I'm doing the same things! I feel happy watching them so I cheer them on.

My dad came home from work one evening and asked, "What did you do today at school?" I told him about watching my friends at recess doing the monkey bars. Next thing I knew, my dad put me in his car. My heart skipped a beat when we ended up at the park...my favorite place! My dad got out of the car and said, "Come on." I followed him. We walked to the monkey bars, he picked me up and helped me hang on them.

My heart was so happy! My dad hears me.
He helps me do new things all the time.
I love my dad!

There are things that are hard for me to do, and things that aren't as difficult. I love to surprise people and myself by learning new things! I can now stay on a swing for more than 5 minutes without my right hand slipping off the chain! All it took was practice..and

I feel free when I'm on the swing!

I can also walk and even run! I may walk slower
than you, but I can go to the same places you go.
It just might take me a little longer to get there.
That is why I wear braces on my feet. They add
a pep to my step so that I can run faster and
jump higher!

I can even ride around on a scooter and keep my right hand on the handlebar!

When I first got my scooter, I loved surprising my parents when I sped off and was way ahead of them! WAHOO!!! I can travel so fast on it, which makes my parents nervous, but I feel like I can rule the world!

Remember those shoes I asked you to put on?
You can take them off now and be you! So you
see, I can do lots of things you can do. I may not
win at a game of tag, be able to climb a tree, or
do a cartwheel...yet. SOMEDAY!

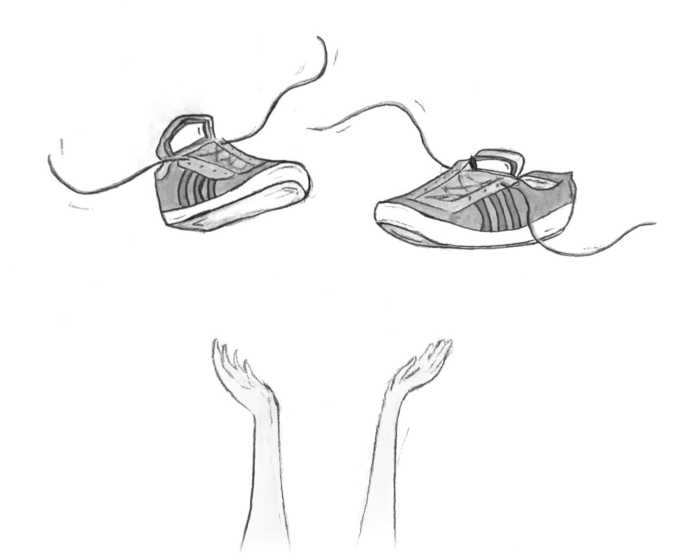

My message to you is, please remember that nobody looks the same, talks the same, walks the same, or dresses the same. If we all did, how boring would that be? Next time you see someone that may act weird or different, or walk or talk funny, please be kind to them. If you put yourself in their shoes, you would learn their story! They may not be able to control how they walk or talk, like you can. Be thankful for being YOU! I am!

One thing I know for sure is this girl's got

grit

I feel extremely blessed to have this opportunity to share Frankie's story, and I hope and pray it's a blessing to you too. Empathy is hard to teach. But my heart's desire is that through this book, children will better understand how to accept and celebrate children like Frankie. Children with unique abilities deserve to be understood and accepted!

I'm often asked questions like, "Why does Frankie wear braces on her feet?" or "Why does Frankie go to therapy?" I sometimes find myself struggling with how to respond. This is when I decided to give Frankie, and other children like Frankie, a voice. This book will help answer some of these questions and hopefully, give you a glimpse into the life of an amazing little girl who's got grit!

Francesca Margo was born in 2010, and our lives felt complete. Despite numerous medical issues she encountered as an infant, we didn't realize how it would affect her future. However, once we knew Frankie was going to need special care indefinitely, my internal dialogue shifted, and I began to dwell on questions like, "Why me? Why us? What could we have done differently to prevent this?"

What helped me tremendously with anxiety was blogging and participating in support groups. I was a little hesitant at first to share my story with others, but I found that the more I did, the less lonely I felt. I allowed myself to be vulnerable and opened up to other parents and caregivers that were in the same boat---I like to call it a cruise ship. The wealth of knowledge and friends I have gained during our journey has been priceless. That's how this book was born!

If you have or know a child like Frankie, we'd love to hear from you. Please visit our website, www.thisgirlsgotgrit.com, and find us on Facebook and Instagram.

"Because of your little faith," he told them.
"For truly I tell you, if you have the faith the size of a
mustard seed, you will tell this mountain 'move from here
to there,' and it will move. Nothing will be impossible for you."

-Matthew 17:20

CPSIA information can be obtained
at www.ICGtesting.com
Printed in the USA
BVHW021927020820
585291BV00070B/87